Ostriches

Victoria Blakemore

vblakemore.author@gmail.com

Copyright info/picture credits

Cover, tratong/Shutterstock; Page 3, anu_johanna/Pixabay; Page 5, ah-layout/Pixabay; Page 7, AJJ74/Pixabay; Page 9, ronbd/Pixabay; Pages 10-11, EcoView/AdobeStock; Page 13, Bluesnap/Pixabay; Page 15, Alexas_Fotos/Pixabay; Page 17, rujhan_basir/Pixabay; Page 19, paula french/Shutterstock; Page 21, a-ria/Pixabay; Page 23; Co-Sch/Pixabay; Page 25, DukeAsh/Pixabay; Page 27, Bluesnap/Pixabay; Page 29, evaschlomberg/Pixabay; Page 31, fxxu/Pixabay; Page 33, tratong/Shutterstock

Table of Contents

What Are Ostriches?

Ostriches are large birds. They are actually the largest and heaviest of all birds. They are related to emus, cassowaries, and kiwis.

There are five different kinds of ostrich. They differ in size, color, and where they live.

Ostriches are black, tan, white, gray, and pink in color. Males have black feathers. Females have gray-brown feathers.

Size

Ostriches can grow to be between five and nine feet tall. When fully grown, they often weigh between about 200 and 300 pounds.

Male ostriches are usually larger than female ostriches. Some male ostriches have been weighed in at over 340 pounds

Physical Characteristics

Ostrich feathers are different from most bird feathers. They are loose and soft. This gives ostriches a furry look.

Ostrich eyes are the largest of any land animal. They are about two inches across. They have very good vision and can see far away.

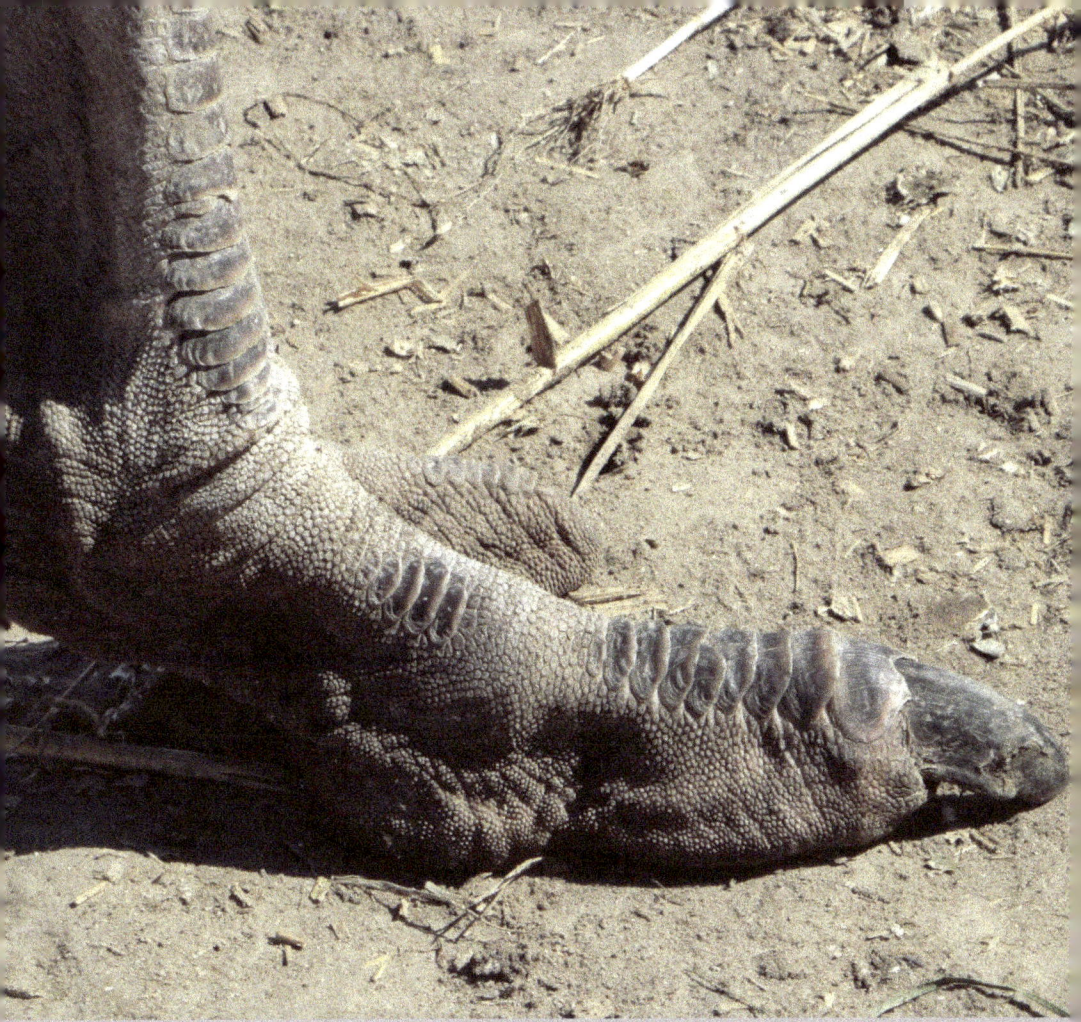

Ostriches are the only birds that

have two toes. One is long and

has a sharp claw. The size and

shape of their feet help ostriches

to run fast. **7**

Habitat

Ostriches are usually found in deserts and savannas. Some have been found in wooded areas.

It is very hot and dry where ostriches live. They are able to survive in high temperatures and with very little water.

Range

Ostriches are only found on

the continent of Africa.

Ostriches are often found in
countries like Kenya, South Africa,
Uganda, Ethiopia, and Sudan.

Diet

Ostriches are **omnivores**. This means that they eat meat and plants.

Their diet is made up of roots, leaves, seeds, insects, lizards, snakes, and small rodents. Much of the water they get comes from the food they eat.

Ostriches are able to survive for several days without water. This helps them to survive in the hot, dry deserts and savannas.

When ostriches eat, they store the food at the top of their throat. When the lump of food is large enough, they swallow it.

Ostriches also swallow sand, pebbles, and small stones. The stones and sand help ostriches to **digest** their food.

The sand and stones stay in the **gizzard**. They move around and help to break down food.

Communication

Ostriches use mainly sound to communicate. They can also use movement. Males often use wing movements to send messages.

Ostriches are able to make many different sounds. They can whistle, snort, snap their bills, and more.

Male ostriches can make a

loud booming sound. It is often

used if a predator is near.

Movement

Although ostriches are birds, their large size and weight make them unable to fly.

They have long, strong legs that help them to run very fast. Their wings are kept open when they run. This helps them balance, especially if they have to turn quickly.

Ostriches can run very fast. They
have been known to run over
forty miles per hour.

Ostrich Chicks

Female ostriches lay up to ten

eggs in a nest made out of dirt.

The male and female ostriches

take turns sitting on the eggs to

keep them warm.

Several ostriches may lay eggs in

the same nest. Ostrich eggs are

very large and often weigh

about three pounds each.

Ostrich chicks hatch after about forty days. They grow very fast and are the same size as their parents in about six months.

Ostrich Life

Ostriches live in groups that are called flocks. A flock often has about ten birds in it.

If ostriches are not able to run and danger is nearby, they fall to the ground. Their head and neck lay flat on the ground. It makes it look like their head is in the sand.

Ostriches can rest by tucking

their legs under their body.

Staying Safe

Ostrich flocks work together

to watch out for predators.

They warn each other if one is

nearby. This helps to keep

them safe.

Although they usually run from

predators, ostriches can use

their sharp claws to **defend**

themselves if they need to.

Ostriches have long necks and good eyesight. This allows them to spot predators from a distance.

Population

Ostriches are not currently **endangered**. There are many left in the wild. However, their numbers have been **decreasing**.

The Somali ostrich is listed as **vulnerable**. It is not known how many are left, but their population has been **decreasing** rapidly.

In the wild, ostriches often live

between thirty and forty years.

Ostriches in Danger

Although ostriches are not **endangered**, they are still facing several threats.

For many years, ostrich feathers were very fashionable. They were often added to hats. Ostriches are still hunted for their feathers, meat, eggs, and fat.

The main threat to ostriches is habitat loss. Their habitats are being destroyed for buildings, roads, and farmland.

29

Helping Ostriches

There are a few ways that people are trying to help ostriches. In some areas, special areas of protected land have been set up. They provide animals like ostriches with a safe habitat.

Some groups are working to get even more land protected for animals like ostriches.

Some groups raise ostriches on farms. When the ostriches are old enough, they can be **released** into the wild.

These groups also teach others how to raise ostriches. Their goal is to continue to **release** ostriches into the wild to help **increase** their populations.

Glossary

Decreasing: getting smaller

Defend: to protect, to keep safe

Digest: to break down food into materials that can be absorbed and used by the body

Endangered: at risk of becoming extinct

Gizzard: an organ that helps birds to break down food using sand or stones

Increase: to get larger

Omnivore: an animal that eats meat

and plants

Release: to set free

Vulnerable: an animal that could

soon become endangered if their

population continues to decrease

Victoria Blakemore is a first grade

teacher in Southwest Florida with a

passion for reading.

You can visit her at

www.elementaryexplorers.com

Also in This Series

Gray Wolves · Sloths · Flamingos · Camels · Koalas · Honey Bees · Pandas

Pangolins · White-Tailed Deer · Orcas · Giraffes · Corn · Meerkats · Echidnas

Walruses · Raccoons · Bald Eagles · Apples · Arctic Foxes · Red Pandas · Cassowaries

Tigers · Ladybugs · Moose · Beluga Whales · Leopards · Elephants · Jellyfish

Binturongs · Lions · Dolphins · Reindeer · Hammerhead Sharks · Hippos · Pumpkins

Peafowl · Chameleons · Florida Panthers · Aye-Ayes · Black Bears · Cheetahs · Manatees

Gingerbread · Polar Bears · Hot Chocolate · Orangutans · Coyotes · Marshmallows · Strawberries

Also in This Series

Aardvarks	Mako Sharks	Alligators	Frogs	Hedgehogs	Brown Bears	Bongos
Sea Turtles	Quokkas	Muskrats	Zebras	Red Foxes	Ring-Tailed Lemurs	Platypuses
Anteaters	Kangaroos	Rhinos	Jaguars	Wombats	Capybaras	Gorillas
Cats	Skunks	Butterflies	Dingoes	Snow Leopards	African Wild Dogs	Penguins
Whale Sharks	Wolverines	Warthogs	Caracals	Badgers	Seals	Hummingbirds
Pikas	Humpback Whales	Pumas	Lemonade	Llamas	Tulips	Ostriches

Victoria Blakemore